Workbook for
The Study of
Orchestration
Third Edition

Workbook for
The Study of Orchestration

Third Edition

Samuel Adler

Professor Emeritus, Eastman School of Music of the University of Rochester
Composition Faculty, Juilliard School of Music

W. W. Norton & Company
New York · London

ISBN 0-393-97700-5 (pbk.)

W. W. Norton & Company, Inc., 500 Fifth Avenue, New York, N.Y. 10110
www.wwnorton.com.

W. W. Norton & Company Ltd., Castle House, 75/76 Wells Street, London W1T 3QT

9 0

Contents

Preface

During the ten years since the publication of The Study of Orchestration, second edition, the response to its workbook has been most gratifying. Many instructors have taken the time to send me suggestions of what to add to a third edition workbook. After considering all suggestions very carefully I have incorporated a great number of them into this new edition. I have increased the number of "Listen and Score" exercises, since they have proven to be very successful. The six new ones, comprising one for strings, one for woodwinds and brass, and four for full orchestra, are by request less complex than the existing ones. I have substituted quite a few new works in the transcription exercises with the aim of introducing the student to a greater variety of composers, including women and minority composers of the past and present. As in previous editions, transcription exercises have been drawn not only from the piano literature but also from the choral, solo vocal, and instrumental repertoire. New to this edition are exercises that require the student to reduce full scores to piano scores. The goal of these exercises is to help the student identify the most important components of the original orchestral passage as well as to recognize each component's doublings and colorations.

The accompanying set of enhanced CDs provides opportunities to examine other strategies for training the ear and mind in the study of the orchestral idiom. The "Test Yourself" exercises have been augmented with computer exercises that deal with range, transposition, string bowing techniques, string harmonics, and harp pedaling techniques. In addition, the student can access a completely new series of reorchestrations of existing orchestral works, which I hope will generate class discussions about the suitability of substituting certain orchestral colors for other ones and the effectiveness of choosing particular combinations of instruments over other ones within an orchestral texture. All exercises—written and electronic—are designed to strengthen the student's orchestral writing techniques.

I urge the instructor to have as many assignments played by live instrumentalists as possible. To this end I have included once again a selection of works to be transcribed for instruments that might be available to an actual orchestration class or for instrumentalists who might be convinced to help out in the class. Assembling heterogeneous ensembles to play through the orchestration exercises has given students enormous insight into orchestral problems.

I realize that many students today have easy access to electronic sound sources; however, since these media do not truly reproduce acoustic instrumental sounds and playing techniques, students are often not well served and are even misled by them. Electronic sounds certainly do not take into account orchestral balance. Only hearing live performances will assure that the student learns about the sound and playing techniques of each instrument, about each orchestral section, as well as how to balance the various sections of the orchestra.

This workbook contains a large number of exercises, all of which cannot possibly be assigned in a semester- or perhaps even a year-long course. However, it has been my experience that the greater the variety of available exercises, the more interesting the music making. I hope that this workbook, which I consider an important companion to *The Study of Orchestration* text, will prove to be a valuable tool for both student and instructor.

Samuel Adler, Spring 2002

Introduction to the Student

A workbook that accompanies a textbook should be like a laboratory where you can hone your skills at will. We have tried to organize this volume with exactly that purpose in mind. There are exercises in transposition, clef reading, and transcribing from other media to orchestra, and exercises that will challenge your ear to hear textures, bowings, and the great variety of orchestral colors. For this new edition, we have even enlarged the laboratory by adding many electronic exercises found on the accompanying enhanced CD set, which also gives videos of the instruments actually performing various orchestral techniques, as well as additional information about the composers whose music is contained in *The Study of Orchestration*.

This indeed is an exciting time to be a student of orchestration, when you can experiment in learning the art in so many ways. We are confident that this workbook and its accompanying enhanced CD set will help you learn orchestrational skills more quickly. Let us utter one word of caution, however: while it is possible to use various software programs to ease the tasks of transposing, reading clefs, and other basic music skills by letting the machine do the work, we urge you not to do this—don't be tempted away from acquiring these skills solidly, in the old-fashioned way. You may find yourself in situations where a computer is not readily available and all you have is the reliability of your skills. There is no substitute for being able to mentally accomplish all orchestrational tasks with your own developing skills.

Orchestration—that is, composing the colors of music—is a very creative art. We have tried to make the process of acquiring orchestrational skills an exciting adventure.

Workbook for
The Study of
Orchestration
Third Edition

Test Yourself I

Strings

1. Name the open strings on each instrument:

    a. violin _____

    b. viola _____

    c. cello _____

    d. double bass _____

2. What is the meaning of *sul D*? _____

3. What is the III string on the viola? _____

4. What is the I string on the double bass? _____

5. What is the II string on the cello? _____

6. What is the IV string on the violin? _____

7. What is meant by *scordatura*? _____

    Give an example. _____

8. What is meant by third position on the violin? _____

_____

_____

_____

9. What is a double stop? _____

_____

10. Why are the following double stops not possible to perform on each designated instrument?

_____

_____

11. Here is a chord progression from Mozart's *Le Nozze di Figaro*. Expand each simple chord into one using double, triple, or quadruple stops for each section of strings. Write triple stops in all places unless otherwise specified (② = double stop; ④ = quadruple stop). Leave the double bass line as single notes, except for the last chord. The first chord is given.

Adagio

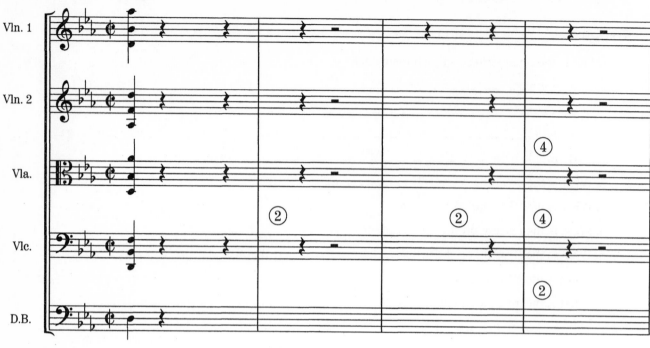

Vln. 1

Vln. 2

Vla.

Vlc.

D.B.

12. Define the following terms that pertain to the bow:

    a. frog _____

    b. heel _____

    c. tip _____

    d. What is the downbow sign?   The upbow sign?

13. What is meant by *portamento*? _____

14. What is the difference between portamento and glissando? _____

_____

15. Explain pizzicato. _____

_____

16. What is left-hand pizzicato and how is it indicated? _____

_____

17. What is the most common designation used to tell string players to put on a mute? _____

_____

18. To take off the mute? _____

19. What is a natural harmonic? _____

_____

_____

20. Write two natural harmonics for each of the four bowed string instruments. (Write the correct notation and what the actual sound will be.)

21. What is an artificial harmonic? _____

_____

22. Write three artificial harmonics for each of the following: violin, viola, and cello. (Write the correct notation and what the actual sound will be.)

23. Describe the difference between the way an artificial harmonic is produced on the

violin and on the cello. _____

_____

_____

24. What is meant by harmonic series? _____

_____

25. Write out the first six overtones for the following fundamentals:

a.   b.   c.

Name _____

Worksheet 1

Clefs

1. Rewrite for viola in alto clef.

2. Rewrite for cello using bass and tenor clef.

3. Rewrite in alto clef.

4. Rewrite in treble clef

5. Transcribe for viola (include bowings).

Quite slowly

6

6. Transcribe for cello (include bowings). Use bass clef and tenor clef only.

1 **Andante con moto**

6

7. Transcribe for violin (include bowings).

1 **Quietly moving**

5

9

8. Transcribe for cello using only tenor clef (include bowings).

9. There are errors in both of the transcriptions given below. Find them, circle them, and rewrite them on the blank staff.

a.

8

Worksheet 2

Bowing

1. Bow all the string parts carefully in both of these excerpts from Handel's *Water music*, Suite No. 1 in F major. You may benefit from listening to recordings of these two movements before you do the actual bowings.

Handel, *Water music*, Suite No. 1 in F major

Overture, mm. 1–12

Air, mm. 1–18

2. Supply three different ways of bowing this passage.

3. Supply two different bowings for this passage.

4. Supply two different bowings for this passage.

a. Vla.

b.

5. Listen to the following complete violin passage, played *non legato*. Then, for each of the twenty different bowings of the passage that you hear on the CD, write the letter corresponding to its correct notation.

CD-6/TR. 71

Allegro moderato

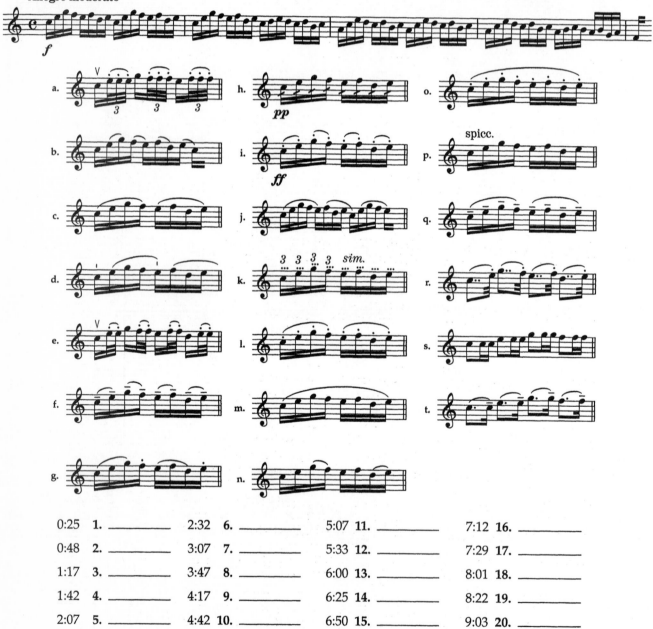

0:25 **1.** _____   2:32 **6.** _____   5:07 **11.** _____   7:12 **16.** _____

0:48 **2.** _____   3:07 **7.** _____   5:33 **12.** _____   7:29 **17.** _____

1:17 **3.** _____   3:47 **8.** _____   6:00 **13.** _____   8:01 **18.** _____

1:42 **4.** _____   4:17 **9.** _____   6:25 **14.** _____   8:22 **19.** _____

2:07 **5.** _____   4:42 **10.** _____   6:50 **15.** _____   9:03 **20.** _____

Worksheet 3

String Harmonics

1. Write the notes that actually sound in this violin passage.

2. Write out the notes that actually sound in this cello passage.

3. Rewrite this viola passage so that every note is played either as a natural or an artificial harmonic.

Worksheet 4

Transcribing for String Orchestra

1. On a separate sheet of manuscript paper, transcribe this passage written for Baroque string orchestra for a modern string orchestra that uses two separate violin parts, a viola part, a cello part, as well as separate bass part whenever you feel it necessary.

● Although your texture will be thicker than the original, you should use the chords that are prescribed by the figured bass and preserve the style.

● Write out the repeats of the first and second strains, using *mf* the first time played and *p* the second. The dynamics should have a direct impact on the way you orchestrate each strain.

Handel, Concerto Grosso, Op. 6, No. 12, Air, mm. 1–28

2. Study this canon by William Boyce and write it out on a separate sheet of manuscript paper as it would be realized by three singing voices. Canonic entrances are indicated by the numbers (1., 2., 3.) above the staff. Then complete the version for string orchestra, most of which is given below.

- Notice that parts have been added to this realization; you don't have to follow the original canon scheme entirely.

- Try to maintain an eighteenth-century style.

Boyce, "Epitaph"

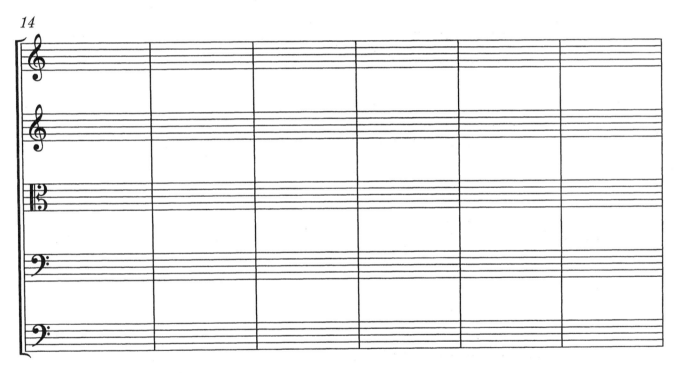

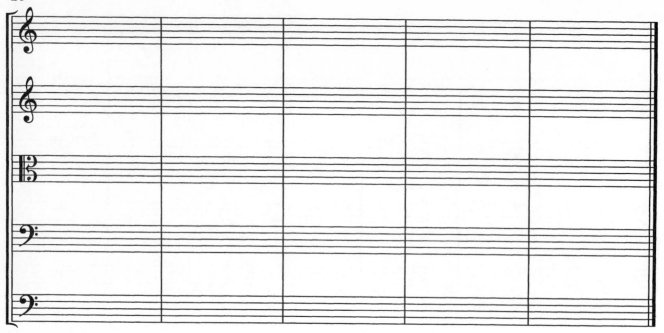

3. On a separate sheet of manuscript paper, continue the arrangement of this canon by Luigi Cherubini in the same manner as we begin it below, making certain that the original melody is heard throughout in one of the voices.

- You may wish to keep the melody in the second violin part all the way through.

- Do keep some independent voice or voices going until the end.

- Notice some elaborations in handling the original tune, for instance, in the viola part (measures 2–3); you may certainly treat the tune freely throughout.

Cherubini, "Solmisation" (three-voice canon)

4. Here are four different harmonizations by Bach of the same chorale tune. Make a different string orchestra version for each of these harmonizations.

- You may transpose the harmonization, put the chorale tune into an inner voice, or vary the original in any other way, but do not change the harmony or the melody.

- Supply dynamics and bowings for each of your orchestrations.

Bach, Four Settings of a Chorale Tune

5. Transcribe the following piece for string orchestra.

- Supply dynamics all the way through.

- You may want to thicken the texture, but don't overdo it.

- Mark the bowings accurately so that the chords come through strong and clear.

Gambarini, *Lessons for the Harpsichord* **(1748), Allegro**

6. Here are two seventeenth-century canons for three voices. Both are given in the original format, in which numbers appear at the end of each voice part to indicate which line to sing next. The first canon has been realized or written out to show how the canonic voices enter (the second voice enters eight measures after the first, and the third voice eight measures after the second).

- Transcribe each canon for full string orchestra.

- Realize the second canon in the same way shown for the first; notice that each voice performs the entire canon of 24 measures, and then voices 1 and 2 repeat the canon until voice 3 has completed all 24 measures.

- You may transpose each piece to any key, and use any octave transposition.

- Supply dynamics and bowings.

J. Cobb, "Hey Ho! Heart's Delight" (ca. 1650)

original format

written-out format

J. Hilton, "Come Let Us All A-Maying Go" (ca. 1630)

original format

Listen and Score 1

Haydn, Symphony No. 100 ("Military"), second movement [CD-6/TR. 26]

- Listen carefully to this orchestral passage, following the piano score given immediately below. You may jot down notes about the orchestration in this score.

- On a separate sheet of manuscript paper orchestrate the passage exactly as you hear it, using the orchestral setup given below.

- Listen carefully to the partially independent double bass part.

- *Hint:* The violas play *div.*

Listen and Score 2

Mozart, Divertimento (K.247), Menuetto   CD-6/TR. 27

- Listen to this excerpt several times, following the piano score given immediately below.
- Transcribe it for five-part string orchestra exactly as you hear it.
- Be sure to include all dynamics.
- Include all articulations that you hear.

Listen and Score 3

Schubert, *Rosamunde,* **Overture** | CD-6/TR. 28 |

- Listen carefully to this passage, and then score it for five-part string orchestra.
- All the pitches are given in the piano reduction, but you may add octaves in the bass.

Listen and Score 4

Beethoven, Symphony No. 3 ("Eroica"), second movement   CD-6/TR. 29

- Score this passage for string orchestra. Some of the pitches may be in a different octave in the piano reduction than what you actually hear on the CD.

- Mark all articulations carefully.

- Supply dynamics.

Adagio assai

Listen and score 5

Tchaikovsky, *Serenade for Strings,* **Waltz** | CD-6/TR. 30 |

- Listen to the excerpt carefully. The piano reduction is pragmatic and may not always reflect the actual octave in which a note occurs.

- Score for string orchestra.

- Supply bowings and dynamics.

- *Hint:* The second violins and violas play some *non divisi* double stops.

Worksheet 5

Harp

1. Give letter and pictorial representations of the pedal settings for the following glissandi above each example:

a.   **b.**   **c.**

d.   **e.**   **f.**

2. Arrange the following two passages so that they can be played on the harp. Use enharmonic spellings to make the pedaling possible. You may need to omit, add, or rearrange notes to make the chords more effective in the harp version.

Piano Version   **Harp Version**

String Version

Harp Version

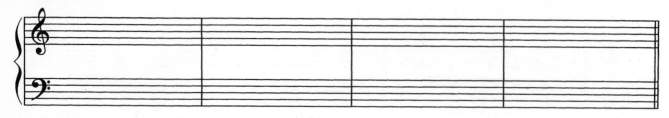

3. What keys do these pedal settings reflect?

a.

c.

b.

d.

Worksheet 6

Transcribing for String Orchestra and Harp

1. Score this prelude by Chopin for strings and harp. Place the harp above the strings in the score.

● You may want to shift the melody an octave or more higher, but remember that by doing so you will give the entire score a different hue. If you decide to do this, try to keep the melody in the original octave for at least part of the piece. Use your imagination.

● Be sure that you carefully follow the dynamics and pedaling of the original; these should influence your resulting orchestration.

Chopin, Prelude in E Major, Op. 28, No. 9

2. Score this piece for string orchestra and harp.

- Retain the texture but make it as orchestrally colorful as possible.

- Use your ingenuity in handling the bass tremolos. You may add octaves up or down, but keep the tremolos very soft.

Liszt, "Nuages gris"

3. Transcribe Bartók's piano piece for strings and harp.

- Use effects such as pizzicato, *col legno*, *près de la table*, and any others you feel are appropriate.

- You may use any octave transpositions.

- The dynamics and registers should give you hints as to the most suitable instrument for a particular solo phrase.

Bartók, *Mikrokosmos*, "Wrestling"

4. Make a very lush arrangement of this Borodin piece for string orchestra and harp.

- Pay attention to the dynamics provided by the composer; since there are so few, you may wish to supply some more.

- You might benefit from listening to Borodin's string writing in some other works before you transcribe this piece.

Borodin, *Petite Suite,* **"Rêverie"**

Test Yourself II

Woodwinds

1. Name the four woodwind families. _____

_____

2. What does the word *embouchure* mean? _____

_____

3. What is meant by overblowing? _____

_____

4. If the sounding pitch is middle C (C^4), what is the written pitch?

   a. alto clarinet   _____

   b. soprano saxophone   _____

   c. D clarinet (piccolo)   _____

   d. E♭ clarinet   _____

   e. C clarinet   _____

   f. tenor saxophone   _____

   g. B♭ clarinet   _____

   h. English horn   _____

   i. alto flute   _____

   j. alto saxophone   _____

5. If the written pitch is middle C (C^4), what is the sounding pitch?

   a. alto clarinet   _____

   b. soprano saxophone   _____

   c. D clarinet (piccolo)   _____

   d. E♭ clarinet (piccolo)   _____

   e. C clarinet   _____

   f. tenor saxophone   _____

   g. B♭ clarinet   _____

   h. English horn   _____

   i. alto flute   _____

   j. alto saxophone   _____

6. What does a slur mean to a wind player? _____

_____

7. Name four ways the player produces vibrato on a woodwind instrument. _____

_____

8. How does one designate a passage to be played without vibrato? _____

_____

9. How is double and triple tonguing achieved on woodwind instruments? _____

_____

10. Describe flutter tonguing. What is the German word for it? _____

_____

_____

11. If two oboes are to play the same part, what is the marking on the score? _____

12. How does one designate the second clarinet to play a passage alone if first and second are notated on the same line? _____

13. Why is the designation *solo* sometimes used? Why is it superfluous? _____

_____

_____

_____

_____

_____

14. What are multiphonics? _____

_____

_____

15. Name some special effects for woodwinds in use today. _____

_____

_____

_____

16. Give the ranges of the following instruments:

a. piccolo   **c.** alto flute   **e.** oboe

b. flute   **d.** bass flute   **f.** English horn

g. All clarinets' written range

i. bassoon

k. oboe d'amore

h. All saxophones' written range

j. contrabassoon

17. Name the first three registers of the clarinet. _____

18. What are the registral characteristics of the following instruments?

   a. flute: _____

   b. oboe: _____

   c. English horn: _____

   d. bassoon _____

19. What is meant by the *break* on the clarinet? _____

20. What can an orchestrator not expect from woodwinds that may be routinely expected from strings? _____

Worksheet 7

Woodwind Transposition

1. Supply the transposition requested in each of the exercises below.

a.

j.

2. Mark an x over, under, or next to all pitch errors in transposition, incorrect accidentals, and outright wrong notes in the two arrangements given below.

Chopin, Nocturne, Op. 37, No. 1, mm. 1–7

Beethoven, Piano Sonata, Op. 27, No. 2 ("Moonlight"), second movement, mm. 8–16

Worksheet 8

Transcribing for Woodwinds in Pairs

1. Complete the canon below, filling in independent parts wherever you would like, as in the first A clarinet part beginning in measure 1.

- Keep the texture as full as possible without changing the style of the piece.

- Supply phrasing and dynamics.

Kuhlau, "Ihr Vögel"

2. Complete the inverted canon in the manner in which it is given below. Thicken the texture without significantly changing the basic harmony.

- All instruments do not necessarily have to play at all times.

- You may wish to write out the repeat in order to vary the instrumental color.

- Supply all phrasing and dynamics.

Brahms, "So lange Schönheit wird bestehn"

Worksheet 9

Transcribing for Woodwinds and Strings

1. Make two arrangements of this American hymn for an orchestral woodwind section of about eight to ten players, the first for woodwinds in pairs, and the second for woodwinds and strings.

● In each arrangement, score for unison melody only in the first sixteen measures (use your imagination when choosing instruments to play); then add in other voices in these measures to flesh out the harmony.

● Try some colorful doublings in each version and differentiate the orchestral colors for each verse of the hymn (starting in measures 1, 17, 33).

D. Read, "Broad is the Road" (ca. 1785)

2. Complete the arrangement of this canon by Brahms in the same manner as it is begun. Then make a second version for the same combination of instruments, retaining a Brahmsian style.

- In your second version you may thicken the texture, if you desire.

- Supply all dynamic, phrasing, and tempo indications in both versions.

Brahms, "Schlaf, Kindlein, schlaf"

61

3. Transcribe this movement for winds in pairs and string orchestra.

- The modern piano part realizes the figured bass and does not have to be retained; however, preserve its basic harmony.

- Be as colorful as possible in your scoring, but do not use all the forces at all times.

- Add in your own dynamic markings, as necessary.

Purcell, Sonata No. 3

4. Transcribe for winds in pairs and strings.

- Use an imaginative foreground-background arrangement throughout.
- Neither the melody nor the accompaniment must remain in the octave given.
- The melody may be doubled or thickened, if desired.

Mozart, Rondo (K. 511), mm. 1–30

5. Arrange this song for winds in pairs, strings, and harp. The melody should remain prominent in your arrangement; however, your transcription should sound more like a work for small orchestra than a song for voice and instruments.

- You may keep the skeletal nature of the harmonic accompaniment or flesh it out either homophonically or contrapuntally; just make sure you retain an early Baroque style.

- Write some solo wind parts with string accompaniment, and on the repeat, at least one solo string passage with wind accompaniment.

- Provide your own dynamics.

R. Jones, "My Love Bound Me with a Kiss"

Worksheet 10

Transcribing for a Large Orchestral Woodwind Section

1. Transcribe this excerpt for a large orchestral woodwind section, making it sound like a large wind band.

- You can add octave doublings anywhere, but do not change the harmony.

- Here you can exploit more extreme dynamic markings, but make sure you orchestrate your fortes differently from your *fortissimos*.

- You can add other pitches at several points, as long as they fit into the harmonic scheme.

Milhaud, *Trois rag caprices*, **Op. 78, No. 1, mm. 1–29**

2. Orchestrate this Debussy prelude for a large woodwind section, strings, and harp.

- Vary the color of the tune in as many ways as possible, but always in good taste!
- Use the harp sparingly so that its appearance is meaningful.
- Use the auxiliary wind instruments (English horn, bass clarinet, contrabassoon, etc.) to good advantage.
- Fill out chords at will, using octave doublings.

Debussy, Preludes, Book I, "La Fille aux cheveux de lin," mm. 1–19

Un peu animé

Listen and Score 6

Mozart, Symphony No. 40 (K. 550), third movement CD-6/TR. 31

- Listen carefully to this excerpt and make notes on the piano score.
- Orchestrate what you heard on a separate sheet of manuscript paper, using the instrumentation given below.
- Mark both phrasings and dynamics.

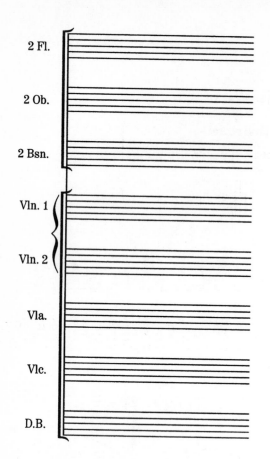

Listen and Score 7

Mendelssohn, Symphony No. 5, fourth movement CD-6/TR. 32

- Listen to the excerpt several times and make notes on the piano version
- Orchestrate the passage as you heard it.
- *Hint:* Orchestrate the obvious parts first and base subsequent decisions on these.

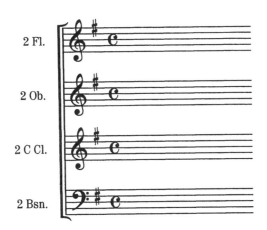

Listen and Score 8

Glinka, *Ruslan and Lyudmila,* **Overture** | CD-6/TR. 33 |

- Listen carefully, then orchestrate what you heard.
- Mark both phrasings and dynamics.

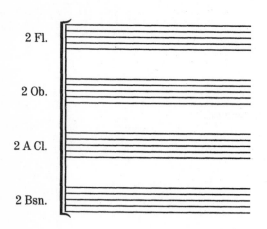

Listen and Score 9

Tchaikovsky, *The Nutcracker* **ballet, Overture**   CD-6/TR. 34

- Listen carefully to the excerpt several times.
- Before scoring, answer these questions:
    1. Is the melody doubled?
    2. Where does the piccolo enter?
    3. Is the first chord in root position or first inversion? How does this influence the scoring?

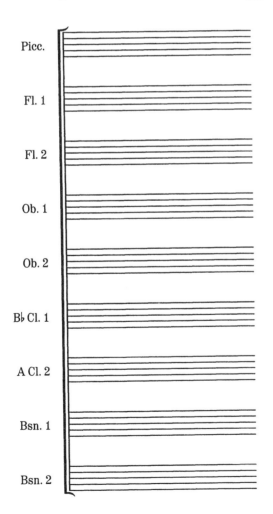

Test Yourself III

Brass

1. Describe the difference between a natural horn or trumpet and a valve horn or trumpet. _____
_____
_____

2. Notate the first seven partials of the harmonic series on F, E♭, B♭, and D.

a. on F

b. on E♭

c. on B♭

a. on D

3. Describe the differences between the trumpet, horn, trombone, and tuba mouthpieces. _____
_____
_____

4. What was the highest partial demanded during the Classical period? _____

5. What is *clarino* playing? _____
_____

6. What is a crook? How does it work? _____
_____

7. What is the difference in the transposition of the F Horn and F Trumpet? _____
_____

8. What does a valve do on a brass instrument? _____

_____

_____

9. Describe what happens when a trumpet player depresses:

    a. the first valve _____

    b. the second valve _____

    c. the third valve _____

    d. the first and third valve _____

    e. the second and third valve _____

    f. the first and second valve _____

    g. all three valves _____

10. What are the positions on the trombone? What effect do they have? _____

_____

_____

_____

11. How many positions are there on the tenor trombone? _____

12. Name the fundamental pitches in all positions on the tenor trombone. _____

_____

13. What are the positions on the bass trombone? _____

_____

14. What note is difficult to perform on the bass trombone unless a G♭ or E attachment is present?

_____

15. What does a mute do to a brass instrument? _____

_____

16. Which is the standard orchestral brass mute? _____

17. Name some other brass mutes. _____

_____

_____

18. What is a Wagner tuba? Name some composers other than Wagner who have used it.

_____

_____

_____

_____

19. What is the major difference between an euphonium and a baritone? _____

_____

20. Name the usual brass complement of a large, modern symphony orchestra. _____

_____

_____

21. What do the designations "B♭ alto horn" and "B♭ basso horn" mean? What is the

transposition of each? _____

_____

_____

22. If the sounding pitch is midde C (C⁴), what is the written pitch for a trumpet

    a. in B♭ _____

    b. in C _____

    c. in D _____

    d. in F _____

23. What is the lowest written pitch for all trumpets? _____

24. Which of the following trills should be avoided on the trumpet?

25. Describe an ophicleide and its sound. _____

_____

_____

26. What is the range of the tuba?

27. What do the pitch designations for the following tubas mean: F, B♭, E♭, C, or BB♭

tubas? Do these instruments transpose? _____

_____

28. How does the diameter of the bell contribute to the sound of the brass instrument?

_____

_____

29. How are horn trills produced? _____

_____

Worksheet 11

Brass Transposition

1. Supply the transposition requested in each of the exercises below.

i.

Sounding

D Tpt.

Written

j.

Sounding

F Hn.

Written

k.

Written

E Hn.

Sounding

Worksheet 12

Transcribing for Woodwinds in Pairs and Horns

1. Transcribe this excerpt for woodwinds in pairs and two F horns.

- You do not have to follow the typically pianistic writing for divided hands.

- For the sustained pitches, choose instruments that can play effective *sforzandos* at the ranges indicated in the original score.

- Reproduce all the dynamic markings in each measure of the score.

- Because some of the extremes in range cannot be replicated by this combination of instruments, you may wish to consider using octave transpositions for the nonsustained parts.

- In handling the repetitive nature of this excerpt, feel free to be as creative in your orchestration as you like.

B. Harbach, "Phantasy and Phugue," mm. 1–6

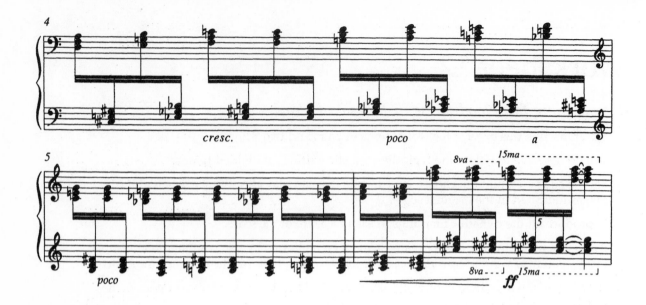

2. Arrange these two Bach chorales for woodwinds in pairs and two horns.

- You may transpose the parts, thicken the texture, and double the melody at will.

- Be sure to indicate your desired phrasing as well as provide tempo and dynamic markings.

Bach, "Heut' triumphieret Gottes Sohn"

Bach, "O Haupt voll Blut und Wunden"

3. Score this piece for woodwinds in pairs and two horns.

- Although you'll want to keep the texture light, don't be afraid to double some of the parts.

- You may wish to transcribe some passages to a higher octave.

- Let the original dynamic markings guide you in choosing your instrumental coloring.

Menotti, "Il Ruscello"

Worksheet 13

Transcribing for Brass

1. Complete the arrangement of Schubert's canon below in the manner in which it is begun. Then, on a separate sheet of manuscript paper, make a second version of it using the same ensemble but orchestrating it quite differently.

Schubert, "Der Schnee zerrinnt"

2. Transcribe each of these two Bach chorales twice: first for 2 horns, 2 trumpets, 2 trombones, and tuba, and then for 4 horns, 3 trumpets, 3 trombones, and tuba.

- In the first version try to retain Bach's harmonic and contrapuntal style, but thicken the texture where you feel it is needed.

- In the second version, use your imagination and create a freer imitative style, reharmonizing any portion of the chorale using your own good taste.

Bach, "Freu' dich sehr, o meine Seele"

Bach, "Was Gott tut, das ist wohlgetan"

3. Transcribe for small brass section (in pairs without tuba).

- You may thicken the texture, but do not add notes that are out of style.
- Be as colorful as you wish in emphasizing the different melodic strains.
- Create your own dynamics by the way you orchestrate the piece.

Bach, *Five Little Preludes* **(BWV 940), No. 2**

Listen and Score 10

Dvořák, Symphony No. 9 ("From the New World"), second movement   CD-6/TR. 35

- Listen carefully to this excerpt and score for 2 E horns (Hn. 1, 2), 1 C horn (Hn. 4), 2 E trumpets, 3 trombones, and tuba.

- Add dynamic and phrase markings, as necessary.

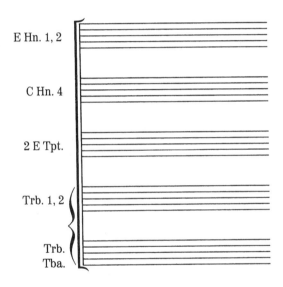

Listen and Score 11

Musorgsky-Ravel, *Pictures at an Exhibition,* **"Promenade"**   [CD-6/TR. 36]

● Listen and then score for 4 F horns, 3 C trumpets, trombone, and tuba.

Listen and Score 12

Berlioz, *Symphonie fantastique*, fifth movement   CD-6/TR. 37

- Listen and then score for 2 E♭ horns, 2 C horns, 2 E♭ trumpets, and 3 trombones.

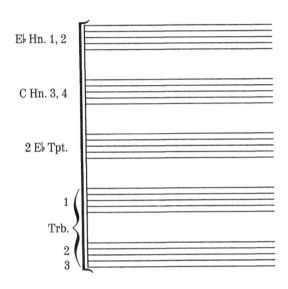

Listen and Score 13

Hindemith, *Mathis der Maler*, **third movement** | CD-6/TR. 38

- Listen and then score for 4 F horns (Hn. 1, 3 on one staff and Hn. 2, 4 on the other), 2
  C trumpets, 3 trombones, and tuba.

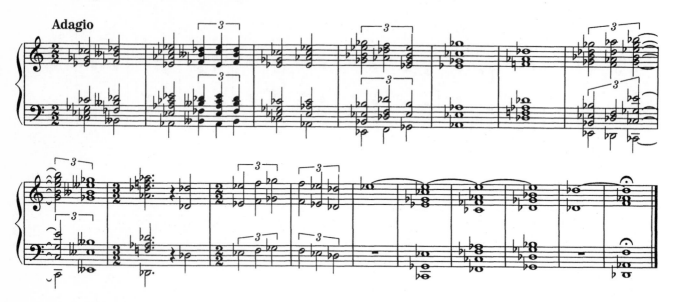

Listen and Score 14

Bartók, *Concerto for Orchestra*, **second movement** ⟦CD-6/TR. 39⟧

- Listen and then score for 4 F horns, 2 C trumpets, 2 trombones, and tuba. Notice that the high horns are on the same staff and begin together.

- Supply the snare drum part, if you can.

Listen and Score 15

Bernstein, *Jeremiah Symphony*, **last movement** CD-6/TR. 40

- Listen and then score for 4 F horns, 3 C trumpets, 3 trombones, and tuba. Notice that the high horns (Hn. 1, 3) are on separate staves, as are the low horns.

Worksheet 14

Transcribing for a Large Orchestral Brass Section

1. Transcribe this excerpt for a full brass section.

- You do not need to thicken the texture, but you may write additional pitches that fit within the given harmony.

- Pay close attention to the dynamics and pedal indications supplied by the composer; these should influence your orchestration.

J. Zaimont, "Jazz Waltz," mm. 1–17

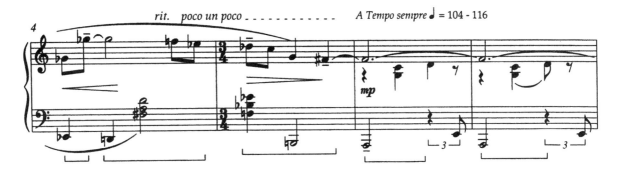

2. Transcribe this excerpt for a large brass section.

- Supply your own dynamics and instrumental spacing, allowing the music to guide your choices.

Stirling, *Romantic Pieces for the Organ,* "Maestoso," mm. 1–26

3. Transcribe this piece for a large orchestral brass section.

- Be sure to keep the melody legato.

- Try to build effective dynamic changes.

- You may thicken the harmony and strengthen the melody with doublings, but do not alter the character of the piece.

Kabalevsky, "Toccatina"

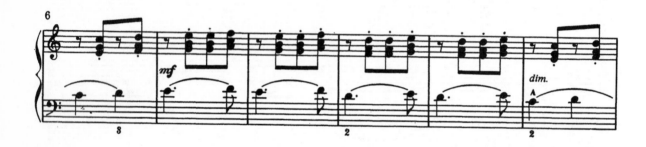

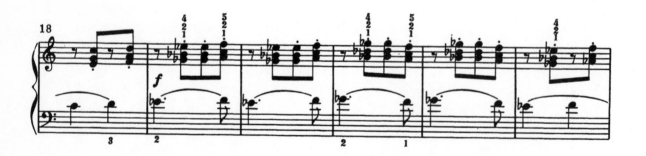

Worksheet 15

Transcribing for Woodwinds and Brass

Complete the realization of this canon by supplying the missing parts and adding independent parts as desired.

- Always stay in the classical style.

- Supply dynamic and tempo markings as well as phrasing indications.

Mozart, "Alleluja" (K. 553)

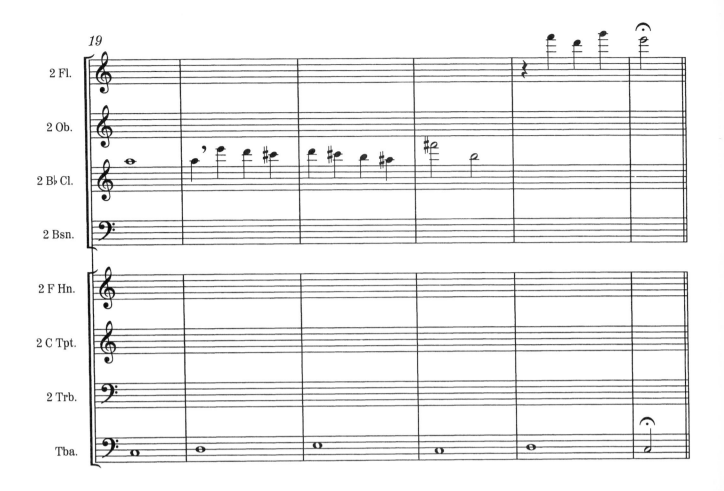

Listen and Score 16

Beethoven, Symphony No. 8, second movement | CD-6/TR. 41 |

- Listen to this excerpt at least five times.
- See how close you can come to the original sound, scoring for woodwinds in pairs (clarinets are in B♭), 2 B♭ horns, and strings.

Listen and Score 17

Mozart, Symphony No. 40 (K. 550), third movement | CD-6/TR. 42

- Listen to this excerpt at least five times.
- Score for 1 flute, 2 oboes, 2 B♭ clarinets, 2 bassoons, 2 G horns, and strings.

Listen and Score 18

Weber, *Euryanthe*, Overture

- Score this excerpt for 2 flutes, 2 oboes, 2 B♭ clarinets, 2 bassoons, 4 horns (B♭ Hn. 1, 2 and E♭ Hn. 3, 4 as originally scored), 2 E♭ trumpets, 3 trombones, and timpani.
- Listen carefully to the doublings, as they can be very tricky.
- The trombones play all the way through.
- Weber uses only two timpani; listen to that part and determine which pitches he uses.

Test Yourself IV

Percussion and Keyboard

1. Define the following terms as they apply to percussion instruments, and then name some percussion instruments in each category.

a. idiophones _____

_____

_____

b. membranophones _____

_____

c. aerophones _____

_____

2. Explain the difference between percussion instruments of definite pitch and those of indefinite pitch. _____

_____

_____

3. What are the various ways to notate percussion instruments? _____

_____

_____

4. What other factors must be taken into account when notating a percussion section in a score? _____

_____

_____

5. Give the percussion layout for the following instruments in a full orchestral score: triangle, xylophone, guiro, glockenspiel, timpani, snare drum, marimba, bass drum.

_____

_____

6. Give the ranges of the following instruments:

a. marimba   b. vibraphone   c. crotales

d. xylophone　　　　　**e.** glockenspiel　　　　　**f.** chimes

g. timpani　　　　　**h.** roto toms

7. Notate the following effects:

   a. four-stroke ruff _____

   b. flam _____

   c. drag _____

   d. roll _____

8. Notate a roll on cymbals or membranophones two different ways.

9. What is the main difference between finger cymbals and crotales? _____

_____

10. What is a slapstick or whip? _____

_____

11. How does one tune timpani? What sizes do they usually come in? _____

_____

_____

12. What are the similarities and differences between tom-toms and timbales? How
many of each can one use? _____

_____

_____

13. What kind of sticks, mallets, or beaters are used for the following instruments:

   a. triangle _____

   b. tom-tom _____

   c. cymbals _____

   d. conga drum _____

   e. crotales _____

14. Describe the cimbalom used in a modern symphony orchestra. _____

_____

_____

15. Give the range of the organ pedals.

_____

16. Give the ranges of the harpsichord and celesta.

    a. harpsichord   **b.** celesta

17. How has the piano been used as a percussion instrument in the last hundred years?

_____

_____

_____

18. Name all the transposing percussion and keyboard instruments and state how they transpose. _____

_____

19. What is a prepared piano? _____

_____

Worksheet 16

Transcribing for Nonpitched Percussion

1. Transcribe the following excerpt for nonpitched percussion.

- Use four percussionists playing a variety of instruments. For instance:
  Player 1 — 5 or 6 temple blocks.
  Player 2 — 2 bongos plus 3 or 4 tom-toms.
  Player 3 — 2 timbales, 3 wood blocks, and a bass or conga drum.
  Player 4 — suspended cymbals and triangles.

- The sustained pedal should be kept as such, but you may color it quite imaginatively.

- Using too many instruments per theme will distort the effect of that theme's statement.

Bach, Toccata and Fugue (BWV 540), mm. 1–83

2. Transcribe for nonpitched percussion using four players. Use instruments similar to those employed for the previous exercise, but in different combinations.

Bach, Prelude and Fugue (BWV 541), mm. 1–38

Worksheet 17

Transcribing for Pitched and Nonpitched Percussion

1. Transcribe for four percussionists.

● Color the "stamp" in various ways, using both nonpitched and pitched instruments; involve the marimba, xylophone, and vibraphone, but never use a simple stamp of the foot.

Joplin, "Stoptime Rag," mm. 1–19

123

2. Transcribe for pitched and nonpitched percussion ensemble of no more than four performers.

Poulenc, *Trois pièces,* "Toccata," mm. 1–27

3. Transcribe this piece for two players using a variety of pitched and nonpitched instruments.

● If necessary, both players should be capable of playing two instruments at the same time in certain places.

Riegger, "Tone Clusters," mm. 1–30

Worksheet 18

Two Transcriptions by Tchaikovsky

Tchaikovsky transcribed two short dances by Mozart, one called Minuet and the other Gigue, and he included them in his Fourth Orchestral Suite titled "Mozartiana." Study Tchaikovsky's transcriptions, each of which is preceded by the original piano piece. Pay particular attention to the skillful and tasteful way in which Tchaikovsky orchestrated these pieces without compromising Mozart's style. Notice also the stylistic orchestral treatment Tchaikovsky gives to both excerpts, particularly his treatment of measures 7–11 in the Gigue.

After studying these pieces, listen to recordings of them, and look also at the piano pieces by Tchaikovsky that Stravinsky orchestrated for *The Fairy's Kiss*. Stravinsky does a masterful job in his transcription, greatly enhancing the music yet keeping the spirit of Tchaikovsky's music intact.

Minuet

Mozart, Menuetto (K.355/576b), mm. 1–23

Tchaikovsky, Suite No. 4 ("Mozartiana"), Menuet, mm. 1–23

Gigue

Mozart, Gigue (K.574), mm. 1–16

Tchaikovsky, Suite No. 4 ("Mozartiana"), Gigue, mm. 1–17

Worksheet 19

Transcribing for Woodwinds in Pairs, Percussion, and Strings

Score this tango for woodwinds in pairs, two percussion players, and strings.

- Use some nonwestern percussion instruments, but do it with good taste.

- You may use octave transpositions, but do not add notes to the already rich harmonies.

- Try to keep Stravinsky's typically lean sound.

Stravinsky, "Tango," mm. 1–24

Worksheet 20

Transcribing for Woodwinds in Threes, Brass, and Percussion

Transcribe this piece for woodwinds in threes, brass, and percussion.

- The percussion section should include timpani and two other percussion players.

- You may also use piano.

- The original dynamics in this work, especially the *sforzando piano* effects, should affect your decisions about scoring.

Dechevow, "The Rails," Op. 16, mm. 1–29

Worksheet 21

Transcribing for Woodwinds in Pairs, Harp, Strings, and Percussion

Transcribe this excerpt for woodwinds in pairs, harp, strings, and one percussion player.

- Color each of the trichords in the right-hand piano part slightly differently.

- Orchestrate the manner in which each trichord is to be played (see the instructions in measures 3–4).

- Be imaginative in your orchestral coloring of the melody.

- Don't overuse the percussion.

- Observe all tempo changes.

Bartók, 14 Bagatelles, Op. 6, No. 7, mm. 1–23

*If there is no *rit.* or *acc.* before the metronome mark, the change of tempo has to be sudden.

**Achievement:

Worksheet 22

Reducing a Full Orchestral score to a Piano Score

Before transcribing piano or vocal works for full orchestra, it is beneficial to become adept at identifying the essential elements of a full orchestral score by reducing that score to a piano score. The orchestrator must be able to isolate the main melodic and harmonic lines from doublings that simply add color and power. This skill will enable him or her to create a piano score of a large vocal or choral work to be used by an accompanist, or a condensed piano score of a concerto or other symphonic work. In addition, it makes the task of orchestrating a piano score much easier to handle.

Here are a few things to keep in mind when creating reduced scores:

● It is not necessary to double notes that are doubled in the full score. Decide on the best sounding octave and stick to it unless the entire piece shifts up or down in range. Try to make your reduction playable by one pianist.

● If the score is so complex that more than two lines are needed for the piano realization, use three or even more staves, as long as one pianist is able to perform your reduction. Many piano pieces composed during the last one hundred years use more than two staves.

● Take note of all transpositions in the full score—for instance, the four horns or the horns and trumpets may be in two different keys. Also, remember that in Mozart, Rossini, and even Beethoven scores the two timpani are notated with C for tonic and G for dominant, no matter the actual key of the piece.* However, you should write the correct pitches in your reduction.

We provide the first few measures for each of the five reduction exercises; copy these measures onto separate manuscript paper before you continue the reductions on your own.

---

* The thinking behind this practice was that the timpani "take on" the bass pitches of the orchestra.

1. Mozart, *Don Giovanni*, Overture, mm. 1–21

Andante

146

2. Rossini, *The Barber of Seville,* **Overture, mm. 1–17**

149

Andante maestoso

3. Beethoven, *The Creatures of Prometheus*, Overture, mm. 1–15

4. Wagner, *Tannhäuser,* **Overture, mm. 142–157**

Tempo I

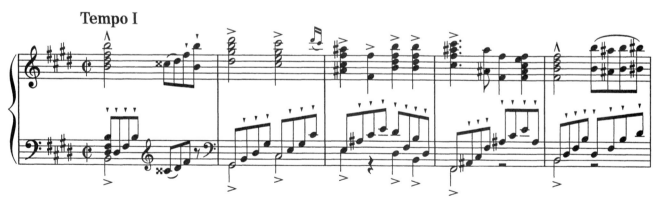

5. Verdi, *Falstaff*, Act II, Scene 1, end, at 25

157

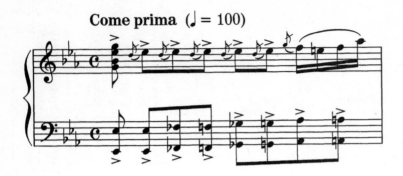

Worksheet 23

Transcribing for Classical Orchestra

Transcribe this piece for a typically Classic-period orchestra, excluding trumpets and timpani:
2 flutes, 2 oboes, 2 clarinets, 2 bassoons, 2 horns, and strings.

- You may thicken the texture, but do not change the harmony.

- You may use octave transpositions and doublings.

Mozart, "Adagio" for Glass Harmonica

Worksheet 24

Transcribing for a Beethoven Orchestra

Transcribe these two excerpts from Beethoven's *Diabelli Variations* for an orchestra used in early Beethoven works: winds in pairs, 2 horns, 2 trumpets, timpani, and strings. In these variations, you will experience orchestrating a tempestuous as well as a calm, melodious Beethoven work. You may wish to listen to some Beethoven symphonies, perhaps the first and fourth movements of the third symphony, in which you will find typical Beethoven treatment of the *sf*.

● Notice the octaves in the second part of Variation 28; give them special and colorful orchestrations.

Beethoven, *Diabelli Variations*

Variation 28

Variation 29

Worksheet 25

Transcribing for a Small Romantic Orchestra

An appropriate instrumentation for this work might be 2 flutes, 2 oboes, 2 clarinets, 2 bassoons, 2 horns, 2 trumpets, 3 trombones, tuba, timpani, two percussion players playing non-pitched instruments, harp, and strings.

● The marchlike, quite fast tempo should influence your scoring.

● Make a pronounced contrast at *soave, e moderato* and provide an effective cadence at the end of the excerpt, even though the piece does not end there.

Moscheles, "La Forza," mm. 21–47

Worksheet 26

Transcribing for Full Orchestra

1. You might wish to listen to the first and fourth symphonies of Robert Schumann before scoring all or part of this piece from this piano work, *Carnaval*.

● Try to imitate the full orchestral sound that he achieves by doublings, but be sure to keep the melody prominent at all times.

● Make a big contrast between the forte and piano sections, just as Schumann does.

Schumann, *Carnaval*, "Valse noble"

2. Transcribe this chorale prelude for full orchestra.

- Be creative in how you color the chorale tune.

- You need not confine the contrapuntal lines to their given registers.

- Observe the dynamic markings in your transcription.

Smyth, "Du, O schönes Weltgebäude!" mm. 1–7

3. This rather sparse piece will really tax your skill as an orchestrator.

- Carefully thinking through the dynamics will help you create your orchestration.
- You may color the pitches using a variety of doublings.
- Retain the sprightly character of this work.
- *Hint:* Remember not all of the instruments need to be used all the time!

Persichetti, Serenade No. 7, "Chase"

4. Score this ragtime two-step for full orchestra.

- In your orchestration, keep the fun in this piece.

- Use the full orchestra very sparingly, but change instrumental colors and textures often.
  You may wish to orchestrate each four-measure repetition within a strain differently.

Joplin, The Strenuous Life, mm. 1–36

Worksheet 27

Transcribing for a Large Impressionistic Orchestra

1. You may wish to study Debussy's *La Mer*, as well as the first two of his *Nocturnes*, before orchestrating this prelude. Then listen to the prelude as it is played on the piano and focus on the sustained long notes, which should influence your orchestration. Imitate as closely as possible the idiomatic style of the composer.

Debussy, Preludes, Book I, "La Cathédrale engloutie," mm. 1–22

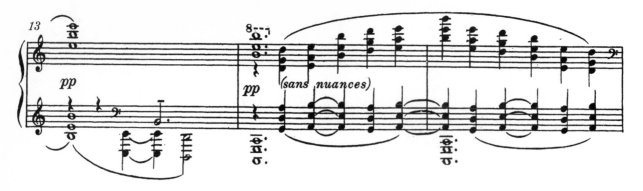

2. Ravel orchestrated many of his own, preexisting piano pieces for four hands and two pianos, such as *Valses nobles et sentimentales* and *Le Tombeau de Couperin*. He did not orchestrate his *Sonatine*, but it lends itself well to that treatment.

- You might wish to study some of Ravel's great orchestral works, such as *La Valse* and his *Daphnis et Chloé*, Suite No. 2, before orchestrating this excerpt.

- The clear melody-accompaniment texture should lead you to treat this piece quite differently from the Debussy prelude.

Ravel, *Sonatine*, first movement, mm. 1–28

Listen and Score 19

Beethoven, *Egmont,* **Overture**   CD-6/TR. 44

- Listen to the excerpt carefully; on first hearing jot down the solo instruments.

- Orchestrate for 2 flutes, 2 oboes, 2 B♭ clarinets, 2 bassoons, 4 horns (F Hn. 1, 2 and E♭ Hn. 3, 4 as originally scored), 2 F trumpets, timpani, and strings.

- See if you can hear exactly what the oboe is doing in the last four measures.

Sostenuto, ma non troppo

Listen and Score 20

Schubert, Symphony No. 8 ("Unfinished"), second movement | CD-6/TR. 45 |

- Listen to this excerpt and score for woodwinds in pairs (A Cl.), 2 E horns, and strings.
- See if you can correctly hear the solo instruments and determine the doublings.

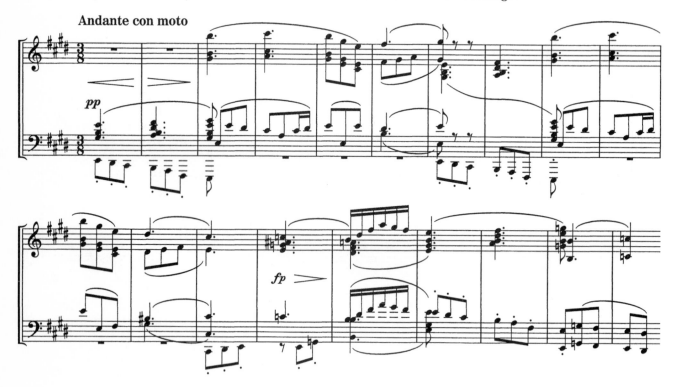

Listen and Score 21

Weber, *Der Freischütz*, Overture | CD-6/TR. 46

- Score this mysterious moment in the overture to Weber's opera for 2 B♭ clarinets, 1 bassoon, timpani, and strings.

- Make certain that you notate the string parts correctly.

Listen and Score 22

Rossini, *La Gazza ladra*, Overture | CD-6/TR. 47

- Orchestrate this excerpt for piccolo, flute, 2 oboes, 2 A clarinets, 2 bassoons, 4 horns, (E Hn. 1, 2 and G Hn. 3, 4), 2 A trumpets, 1 bass trombone, timpani, snare drum, bass drum, and strings.

- Though the orchestration of this excerpt is quite straightforward, some of the doublings are tricky; some chord tones appear only in the trumpets.

- In some places the dotted eighth/sixteenth-note pattern appears only in the brass while straight quarter-note values are played by some other instrumental sections; listen carefully to determine who plays which rhythmic pattern.

Maestoso marziale

Worksheet 28

Transcribing for an Orchestra of Any Size

Transcribe this excerpt for an orchestra of any size.

- Try various ways of bringing out the subject, such as octave or double-octave doublings by instruments of different choirs, pseudo-Klangfarben methods, putting entire choirs on single pitches, and so forth.

- Make certain there is great textural variety.

- Supply all dynamics, phrasing, bowing, and tempi indications.

Bach, *Musical Offering*, **"Ricercare a 6," mm. 1–43**

Worksheet 29

Transcribing for Clarinet and Small Orchestra

This piano piece has an obvious melody and an obvious accompaniment. Arrange the melody in an effective octave for the clarinet soloist and the accompaniment for a small classical orchestra.

Mendelssohn, *Kinderstücke*, **Op. 72, No. 4**

Worksheet 30

Transcribing for Trumpet and String Orchestra

Transcribe this excerpt for B♭ or C trumpet solo and string orchestra, choosing an appropriate key for the solo instrument's range.

- You may thicken the texture of the accompaniment.

- You may change the octave in which the piano part is realized to make the strings sound more effective.

Tartini, violin sonata, Op. 1, No. 12, first movement, Adagio (also published for viola)

Worksheet 31

Transcribing for Flute, Two Oboes, and String Orchestra

Transcribe the viola part into an effective flute register.

- You might wish to change the key of the piece in your transcription.

- Do not change the basic harmony, but don't feel obligated to adhere to the register of the piano realization.

Vivaldi, "Giga," mm. 1–13

Worksheet 32

Transcribing for Voice and String Orchestra

Transcribe these two Bach chorales, the first for soprano, the second for tenor and strings.

- Keeping the basic harmony intact, try to invent figuration that will sound like accompaniment.

- You may transpose either chorale to a different key if necessary, but do not change the tune for any reason.

Bach, "Ein' feste Burg ist unser Gott"

Bach, "Ich dank' dir, lieber Herre"

Worksheet 33

Transcribing Vocal Accompaniments: Small Orchestra

1. Transcribe this piece for a small orchestra of your choosing.

● You may wish to double the melody.

● Your accompaniment does not have to stay in the octave of the original.

● Pay special attention to the tessitura of the voice so that the orchestra will never drown it out.

Dowland, "Behold a Wonder Here," mm. 1–17

2. Orchestrate the accompaniment of this song for an orchestra of woodwinds in pairs, two horns, and strings.

- Make sure you alter your orchestration when the mood and the tempo change in measure 21.

- You may use any octave transpositions, but do not change the harmonies.

Beethoven, "Freudvoll und Leidvoll"

Worksheet 34

Transcribing Vocal Accompaniments: Medium-sized Orchestra

Transcribe this excerpt for a medium-sized orchestra.

- Include the piano pedal effects in your orchestral transcription.

Fauré, "Ici-bas," mm. 1–18

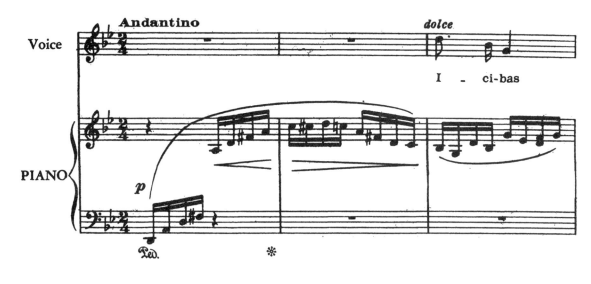

Je rê_veaux é_tés qui demeurent tou_jours!

I_ci-bas les lè_vres ef_fleu_rent Sans rien laisser de leur ve_

_lours, Je rê_ve aux bai_sers qui demeu_rent tou_

_jours.

Worksheet 35

Transcribing Vocal Accompaniments: Large Orchestra

Transcribe this excerpt for a large orchestra.

- Keep the sustained chords of the accompaniment in their given register, but use your imagination in coloring them.

R. Strauss, "Ruhe, meine Seele," Op. 27, No. 1, mm. 1–21

See - le,   dei - ne Stür -me gin - gen   wild, _____ hast ge-

Worksheet 36

Transcribing Vocal Accompaniments: Woodwinds, Two Horns, Harp, Percussion, and Strings

Transcribe this excerpt for woodwinds, 2 horns, harp, percussion, and strings.

● Score for as many percussion instruments (for one player) as you desire.

Debussy, *Trois mélodies*, **"Le Son du cor s'afflige," mm. 1–23**

Worksheet 37

Transcribing for Chorus, Brass, and Strings

Transcribe this excerpt for chorus, brass, and strings.

- You may double the voice parts in the orchestra, but be careful not to overshadow the voices.

- Don't use both brass and strings all the way through.

Monteverdi, "Gloria patri," mm. 1–15

12

Worksheet 38

Transcribing Choral Accompaniments: Medium-sized Orchestra

Transcribe this choral piece for chorus and medium-sized orchestra.

● You may add instrumental doublings, but do not change the harmony.

"Ye Watchers and Ye Holy Ones" (German Melody, ca. 1623)

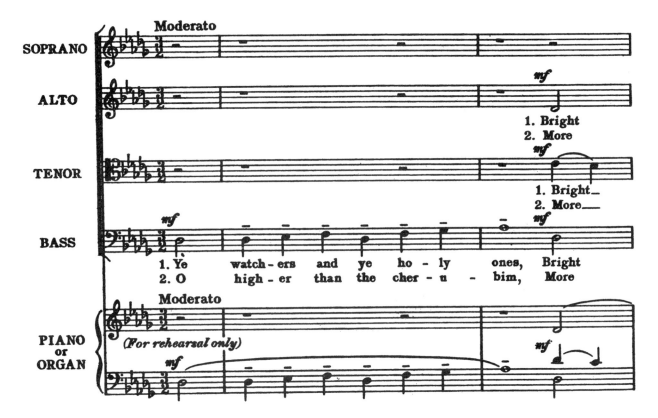

Worksheet 39

Transcribing Choral Accompaniments: Medium-sized Orchestra and Harp

Transcribe the choral accompaniment for medium-sized orchestra and harp.

- You may also wish to double the voice parts at times.

Schubert, "The Lord is My Shepherd," arr. by Sir John Stainer, mm. 1–21

77383-12

Worksheet 40

Transcribing for Available Combinations of Instruments

Transcribe the following six excerpts for any combination of instruments available in your orchestration class. Consider the strengths and weaknesses of each performer for whom you are writing.

- If you use a piano, create an independent part for it and not just a reduction of the score.

- Even if you do not have many instruments at your disposal, make sure that you cover all the pitches and that you use all the instruments at hand to make the score as colorful as possible.

1. E. Hardin, Lesson I, mm. 1–19

2. R. Eubanks, Five Interludes for Piano, No. 2

214

3. Mendelssohn, *Songs Without Words*, Op. 19, No. 1, mm. 1–15

4. Haydn, Symphony No. 103 ("Drum Roll"), third movement, mm. 1–27

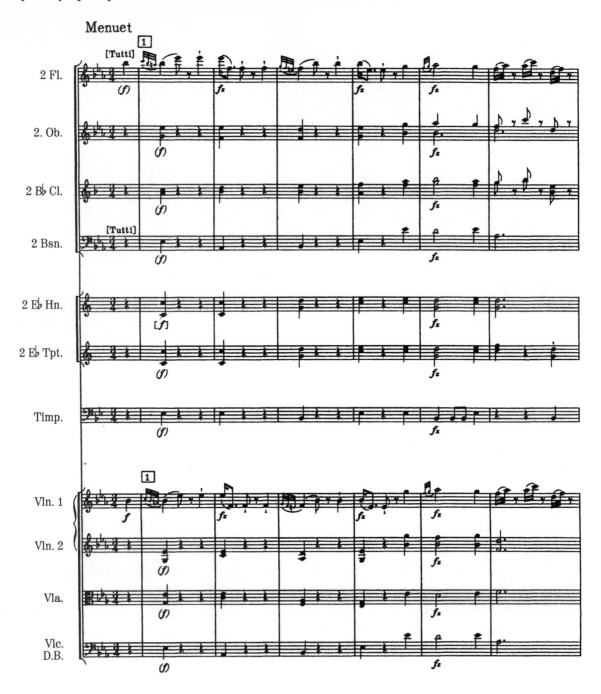

5. Beethoven, Seven Bagatelles, Op. 33, No. 7

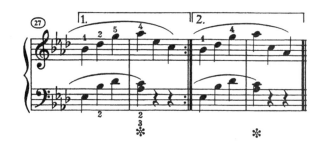

6. Schubert, Quartet in D Minor (D. 810), third movement, mm. 1–41

Worksheet 41

Transcribing for Student Orchestras

Transcribe the following piano pieces for either or both of these ensembles:

a. a junior high school orchestra;

b. a high school or other nonprofessional orchestra.

The junior high score should include a Violin 3 part but no oboes or bassoons. The score for the older group may contain parts for all the instruments in the symphony orchestra.

● You may wish to create miniature concertos out of some of the pieces if there is an especially good instrumentalist in the class.

1. Haydn, Divertimento, Hob. XVI-9, third movement

2. Mozart, Menuett (K. 2)

3. Clementi, Sonatina, Op. 36, No. 1, first movement

4. Bartók, *For Children*, Vol. 2, No. 3

5. Villa-Lobos, *Guia prático, O ciranda, o cirandinha*

Listen and Score 23

Berlioz, *Symphonie fantastique*, **fifth movement** | CD-6/TR. 48 |

- Score this excerpt for 2 timpani and strings divided in this manner: three first violin parts, three second violin parts, two viola parts, and in the last two measures, independent cello and bass parts.

- See how close you can come to Berlioz's orchestration in scoring these divided strings.

- *Hint:* the third first-violin part and the first second-violin part cross each other in contrary motion.

Listen and Score 24

Humperdinck, *Hänsel und Gretel,* **Overture**   CD-6/TR. 49

- Orchestrate this excerpt for 2 flutes, 2 oboes, 2 B♭ clarinets, 2 bassoons, 4 F horns, 3 trombones, timpani, and strings.

- On first hearing mark the solo passages in the reduction; on second hearing mark other details; then copy out the score in its entirety.

- The bassoon parts are so important that we have placed some of their lines in the top line of the reduction. This should help clarify the orchestration.

- Notice the sequence beginning in the thirteenth measure of this excerpt, signalled by the flutes' high C (C[6]) and the canon started by the clarinet. If you mark this early in the listening process it will help you clarify the entire second half of the excerpt.

- This sequence features strong interplay between the trombones and the woodwinds.

- You may wish to notate the horns and strings all the way through and then listen for what roles all the other instruments play.

Listen and Score 25

Mendelssohn, Symphony No. 4 ("Italian"), last movement CD-6/TR. 50

- Score this excerpt for woodwinds in pairs (A Cl.), 2 E horns, 2 E trumpets, timpani, and strings.

- Try to hear the individual colors distinctly.

- Notice that the orchestral texture changes considerably in the last three measures.

Listen and Score 26

Musorgsky-Ravel, *Pictures at an Exhibition*, "Gnomus" | CD-6/TR. 51

- Orchestrate this excerpt, seeing how close you can come to replicating Ravel's scoring.

- Score for 3 flutes, 3 oboes, 2 B♭ clarinets, bass clarinet, 2 bassoons, contrabassoon, 4 F horns (only Hn. 1 and 3 are playing), 1 C trumpet, tuba, timpani, xylophone, and strings.

Listen and Score 27

Musorgsky-Ravel, *Pictures at an Exhibition*, **"Ballet of the Chickens in Their Shells"**

CD-6/TR. 52

- Listen carefully to these eight measures and score for 2 flutes, 2 oboes, 2 B♭ clarinets, 1 bassoon, cymbal, harp, and strings.

Index of Works